Knitting Is Witchcraft

By: Fayte Shuck

& Larisa Hunter (contributor)

TLS

ISBN13: 978-1-959350-67-5

Set in: Georgia 14pt, Marker Felt 36pt, Bodoni 72 Oldstyle 11/14pt, Bodoni 72 Smallcaps 11/14pt, Bookman Oldstyle 11/14pt, Freaky Halloween [Objects/Glyph]

©The Three Little Sisters
USA/CANADA

TO MY GRANDMOTHER CATHY. FOR WITHOUT HER
ENCOURAGEMENT AND JOY OF WRITING I WOULD OF NEVER HAD
THE ABILITY TO WRITE

CONTENTS

LEGEND	
	KNIT
	CROCHET
	CROSS STITCH

GLOSSARY

K	KNIT
P	PURL
K2TOG	KNIT TWO TOGETHER
M1	MAKE ONE (I USE KNIT THROUGH THE BACK LOOP FOR ALL MY M1'S BUT YOU CAN USE WHICH EVER M1 YOU FEEL COMFORTABLE USING)
CO	CAST ON
BO	BIND OFF

CH-CHAIN	
ST(S)	STITCH(ES)
SL ST OR SS	SLIP STITCH
SC	SINGLE CROCHET
DC	DOUBLE CROCHET
HDC	HALF DOUBLE CROCHET
TR OR TRC	TRIPLE CROCHET
DTR	DOUBLE TRIPLE CROCHET
TRTR	TRIPLE TRIPLE CROCHET
QTR	QUADRUPLE TRIPLE CROCHET

THIS BOOK IS DESIGNED FOR INTERMEDIATE TO ADVANCED CRAFTERS

INTRODUCTION

Magic is the art of taking the ethereal and making it material. You do this in a myriad of ways; through prayer, chanting, spells, potions, incantations, and ancestral veneration. You do this too with knitting. You read a cryptic pattern in a neo-modern code, with one or two wands you cast the threads of fate and create the ethereal (what you see in the mind's eye) into the material (what you see on the physical plane).

I believe there is a correlation between why we say cast spells and cast on to start a knitting project both alter the threads of time, space, and fate. The future outcome is based on skill and intention. To the person reading this ...it is your birthright we are all magickal. We are all born with magick. No one begins more magickal than the other. It is a skill you hone over time into a practice.

I once heard it takes 5000 hours to become an expert. I believe this is true if you do the work and practice the skill it becomes second nature. If we based things on pure academia I have 21 years of witchcraft research, However I believe you must practice what you learn in all things you do. So to rephrase I have 3 years active witch practice where I've picked up "the craft" and started doing.

It was easier for me to knit. It has a set rubric with room for alteration based on need, learning style, skill, and purpose of creation. Each stitch tells a story and has a purpose in the overall creation of the item or garment. I have 16 years of knitting experience. I have honed my craft with over 5000 hours of creation. I still see myself as an amateur forever learning new techniques and stitch patterns. I believe the only right and wrong way to knit is on which side of the pattern you like more. We must trust our inherited wisdom and ancestral gifts.

Decolonize is a word we hear a lot lately and I'd like to touch on it in reference to the art of knitting, crocheting, weaving, spinning, and nalbinding. Though I'm only an expert on knitting (though still very much an amateur and novice) I can say this; Trust your ancient wisdom. Deep down we all have an ancestral craft. The British way of colonization does not diminish or remove how to do said craft.

I knit my way because it works for my neurodiverse brain. That does not mean that it is the only way. Trust your wisdom. I teach you what is freely given to me and I hope you do the same. There is no need to create for profit. This is not what this book is. It is a way for you to challenge colonial beliefs and do something solely for the art of creation; and you my friend are a powerful being.

Do not mistake this advice for a vow of poverty or charity. Make! That! Money! If this is the only technical skill you have (and yes it is a technical skill), then use it to get out of debt. You are worth it! To be able to actually revel in life and thrive doing something you love, is a privilege. I only ask you, do not make it your priority to make money from your craft. Remember you can simply exist and enjoy things without making profit.

I learned to knit at a tumultuous time in my life. I will not get into it here but do know it caused a lot of lifelong trauma. My friend saw me struggling and started teaching me the basic stitches to alleviate some of my mental turmoil. Those days eating lunch in my middle school library and knitting are some of my fondest academic memories. Since then I continue to knit to save myself from mental unrest. However, I also knit for the joy of knitting. **For once there was pain I found joy**.

Knitting has become my life line to my past present and future self. I am grateful for the patience and kindness I received from the pool of spiritual mentors who found me, for at the time, I could not be kind to myself or anyone around me; this life preserver, of knitting kept me going. Now in my 30's I'm thriving. I promise you it gets better. Not always physically but mentally...one day you will thrive. **For it once caused pain you now see triumph**. As you begin your journey, I am with you, your ancestors are with you, everyone who's ever picked up 2 needles is with you. You are a stellar being reveling in the sheer awesomeness of creation.

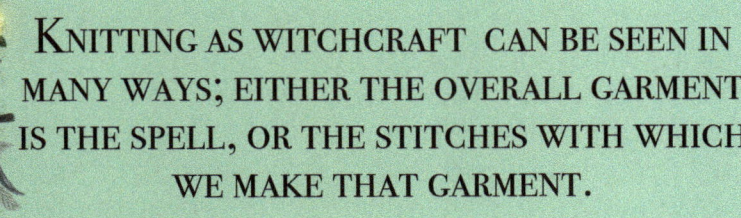

KNITTING AS WITCHCRAFT CAN BE SEEN IN MANY WAYS; EITHER THE OVERALL GARMENT IS THE SPELL, OR THE STITCHES WITH WHICH WE MAKE THAT GARMENT.

ANCESTORS

Recently I got to read the private investigative notes on my great great grandmother on my mothers side.I have found many things. Firstly I am slavic meaning I come from Eastern Europe. Specifically Ukraine (my gedo or grandfather) and Czechoslovakia (my baba or grandmother) when it was part of the Austrian Hungarian Empire. To make matters more interesting, my Grandfather was not only Ukrainian but quite a few years Grandma's junior. This was also my grandma's second marriage. Why is this important? Well people talk a lot about ancestral trauma, why not ancestral gifts? I want to focus on my slavic great great grandparents gifts as i never met them and Im only 3 generations removed from them.

My 4th great grandparents were master weavers on my Grandmother's side. This would explain my affinity with textiles (or as my mom says watching Grandma Ida and Oma Heidi knitting and crochet must have rubbed off on me in my formative years) . I like to think it's much more ingrained than that. I picked up textiles like a fish took to water with very little guidance and training. On my grandfather's side we were potters. Funnily enough I found pottery and excelled in hand building (I still find the wheel tricky).

Though I put down the clay, I'm still active in fibre arts. I did not learn these skills from my family but had an innate knack for them. This may sound like woo but that talent had to come from somewhere and I like to think it was a mixture of ancestral gifts and general interest in the crafts. I now teach knitting with no formal training just a talent and drive gets me classes. From a feverish beginning to an astounding revelation of family inheritance I'd say that is a wonderful ancestral gift. Someone was a weaver of textile artists in all our DNA. Tap into it. Again like magic the skill of creation is your birthright. Use it!

Ancestor veneration is a huge part of my practice both magically and through my fibre creation. I honor my ancestors each time I choose to work with textiles. If you are new to the craft this is a great place to start. We all come from somewhere. We all come from a homeland full of ancient and beautiful textile and pre colonial beliefs. I am predominantly Slavic and Appalachian (we have been in America a long time). These are both deeply rooted in my being. Even though I grew up in the PNW of Washington and British Columbia my DNA has not forgotten my birthright and ancestral teachings, and yours hasn't either. We just have to wake it up. So here's your first magical craft.

ANCESTRAL VENERATION

1 white votive candle (pillar, tea light, 7 day candle, taper, or birthday candle)

*I use ancestral eyes ancestor candle but any white or beeswax candle will do

A glass of water

Your voice

Start with lighting your candle or if you can't have fire in your home an electric candle is fine.

Next call upon your honorable ancestors (these are the ancestors you want to work with not the ones who caused harm) Choose any words you like just state you wish to work with your honorable ancestors.

Place a glass of water next to the candle and inform them this is for them. Use polite and respectful language but ultimately talk to them as if they are a fond relative or friend . And do just that, talk to them for however long you want.

It's important you don't ask for gifts or services right away you want to build a relationship with them. Let them know you're excited to meet them. Tell them about your day to day. Talk to them as long as you need to. I like to sit and knit with mine but that's just me.

When you are ready I extinguish my candle with my breath because they are a part of me (or switch off the candle if it's electric). This symbolizes your time for chatting is over. Leave the water with the candle all day if you like or pour it into a house plant or somewhere in nature. The energies imbued in your ancestor water works wonders on plants. Just saying.

Now go about your day you can now contact them whenever the feeling strikes.

A note on ancestors

Maybe your family sucks and you're from a long line of sucks. That's okay let your found family, your friends, community, crafters, witches and or magic users be your ancestors. There are no real rules in this. If you come from a specific lineage or practice make sure to honor them appropriately for your tradition.

I'm much more of a fly by the seat of my pants witch and work intuitively, but as I learn more about Slavic and Appalachian magical practices I'll incorporate that more into my practice and follow their rule books, but today is not that day comrade and tomorrow well let's just wait for tomorrow.

What is wool?

Wool is fibre taken from the coat or fur of animals such as; sheep, alpaca, rabbit and other animals. This fibre is taken ethically in that it is removed generally through the process of 'shearing' or combing and cutting the fur off the animal in question. This process **does not hurt** the animal at all. In fact, for sheep in particular, shearing helps reduce the weight on a sheep and also helps relive itchiness. There are many varieties of wool, but for this book we will focus on just 10 which are used in various ways, but are the more 'common' types.

⤙Virgin Wool: lambswool. Taken from the sheep's first shearing, this being the softest coast a sheep will ever produce.

As we knit each garment, think of what you want that garment to represent to the recipient. Is it a sweater for courage and confidence? Or maybe a blanket to give strength to a loved one that's ill? Really think of what your intention is behind the garment. Visualize how that person will feel while you knit the garment. Meditate on what the outcome should be once the person has received it.

⟿Merino Wool: specifically from merino sheep (a breed which originated in Spain, but now bred in Australia and New Zealand). It is known for being soft on the skin, temperature regulating and is naturally antibacterial material, repeals unpleasant odor, wicks moisture.

⟿Shetland Sheep: itchy wool, made mostly from Scottish sheep, a durable wool generally used in crating thicker product, a durable wool, made from the undercoat of sheep

⟿Cashmere: come from the undercoat of the cashmere goat, a fine wool, generally used in making very light garments.

⟿Mohair: goat wool, from an Angora goat, thicker than cashmere, it's fiber scales are less prone to tangling and shrinkage. Mohair is generally used in suits and dresses.

⟿Alpaca Wool: the alpacas are native to South America, this soft wool can become itchy in some cases, the fibers are larger and a bit thicker.

⟿Llama Wool: a relative to Alpaca, Llama wool is a very rough wool, generally used in outwear, rugs and décor.

⟿Vicuña: a relative of the llama and alpaca, the vicuña produces rarest wool. Traditionally used by the Incas, reserved for royalty, this wool is warm and soft. Due to conservation concerns, this wool is only shorn every other year.

⟿Qiviut: a wool obtained from the arctic muskox which resides in Canada and Alaska. Harvested during molting season, breeders comb or collect the wool from the ground. It is extremely soft, and very strong, resisting shrinking when immersed in water.

⟿Melton Wool: If you're on the hunt for the best type of wool, Melton wool should definitely be at the top of your list! It's incredibly strong, durable, and super warm, making it perfect for all sorts of cozy garments. Plus, with its thick fibers, it can be woven into a lovely twill-type weave, adding a nice touch to any fabric. You'll love how versatile and reliable it is!

⟿Worsted: Worsted wool is on the pricier side because it's super high-quality. It comes from sheep's wool and is known for being stronger and more versatile than other types of wool. If you're looking for something durable that holds up well, this is a great choice!

⟿Woolen Wool: Woolen wool is a lovely home-spun yarn that's made from soft, stretchy, and lightweight carded wool. It's fantastic at keeping you cozy because it has great insulation properties, making it the perfect choice for all your knitting adventures! You'll love how easy it is to work with!

~Tropical wool: great for use in warmer climates, it comes from merino wool, has great thermal management, which feels cool on your skin.

~Recycled wool: also known as"reclaimed wool," gives new life to leftover materials. It's made from wool used in other products, a second chance as new items. The recycling process might create a lower quality product, but by reusing wool, especially artificial forms, can help reduce environmental impacts of commercial wool manufacturing.

~Raw wool: simply wool in its natural state! It hasn't been processed or refined. Generally, this wool cannot be used 'as is' but some pagans and heathens do use raw wool in creating 'offerings' to deities. There are some artists who have been blending 'raw wool' into woven pieces to create a textured appearance.

~Boiled wool: made by knitting pieces together to create a thick, uniform fabric. Wool threads, are placed on a loom and then run through a weaving machine, creating different colors and textures.

~Felted wool: made from fibers sourced from animals. The wool is cleaned and carded, which breaks it up into manageable pieces. Often used to create dimensional pieces (felted dolls for example).

ARTIFICIAL WOOL

Artificial wool has become a popular choice for crafters out there. It has a generally soft texture while not relying on animals to provide the materials. This wool can contain chemical dyes that may affect sensitive skin. This wool is generally the most 'commonly' available.

~Acrylic Wool: is one of the most common types of artificial wool. It's soft, lightweight, and comes in a ton of colors! Often cheaper than natural wool, easy to care for and machine washable, the wool is great for any kind of project.

~2. Polyester Wool: is a popular choice, especially for those who want something durable, wrinkle resistant and is the closest to the texture of regular real wool, without the itch.

~Nylon Wool: is a strong and stretchy wool, ideal for garments. It's often blended with other fibers to create fabrics which are comfortable and durable.

Rayon Wool: made from regenerated cellulose fibers, making it eco-friendly, is soft and drapes beautifully, making it a favorite for garments. It does require more delicate washing, due to the fragile nature of the fibers.

5. Blended Wool: combines artificial fibers with natural ones to create a fabric which blends the best of both worlds. When looking at textile tags, you will often see a mix of acrylic with natural wool to create the same softness and warmth of natural fibers while enjoying the low maintenance and vibrant colors of synthetic ones.

How is Wool Processed?

The processing of natural wool and artificial wool differs significantly, due to the source of wool and the methods involved in creating each type. Natural fibers take longer to dye than synthetics for example.

Natural Wool Processing

1. Shearing: Natural wool comes from animals like sheep. The wool is carefully shaved off the sheep, during warmer months. Once the wool is sheared, it's sorted and graded based on quality. Wool can contain different fibers, debris, and impurities. The best quality wool is separated between premium wool used for fine garments, and standard wool for general use.
2. Washing (Scouring): After sorting, the wool is washed to remove dirt, grease, and lanolin (a natural oil). It often involves hot soapy water and multiple rinses to ensure the wool is clean.
3. Carding: After washing, the wool is carded, carding is a process, which teased apart and aligned into a fluffy layer, separates the fiber and helps making the wool ready to spin.
4. Spinning: The carded wool is spun into yarn. This is done by twisting the fibers together to create a continuous strand of yarn, which can be made into various thicknesses and textures.
5. Dyeing: If desired, the wool yarn can be dyed using natural or synthetic dyes, giving it a specific color or shade.
6. Finishing: the yarn or fabric may undergo a finishing process, which might include; felting, brushing, or adding treatments to enhance its natural properties.

ARTIFICIAL WOOL PROCESSING

Artificial wool, is made from synthetic fibers like acrylic, polyester, or nylon. The process begins with sourcing these raw materials, which are derived from petrochemicals or other industrial processes.

1. Extrusion: The raw materials are melted down and extruded through spinnerets (think of them like shower heads). This process creates long strands of fiber which can be adjusted in thickness and texture.
2. Cooling and Spooling: After extrusion, the fibers are cooled and solidified. Once set, they are wound onto spools for further processing.
3. Carding and Spinning: Similar to natural wool, the synthetic fibers are carded and spun into yarn. Unlike natural wool, synthetic wool is processed more quicker as the strands are a bit more uniform.
4. Dyeing: The yarn is dyed in the same process as natural wool, either before or after it's spun, using various dyeing methods.
5. Finishing: The final step may include various finishing processes, making the fibers more soft or durable, as well as treatments to ensure different effects such as creating waterproof or stain resistant yarn.

KEY DIFFERENCES BETWEEN NATURAL AND SYNTHETIC WOOL

Natural wool is sourced from animals, while artificial wool is made from synthetic materials. Sometimes the synthetic materials are not exactly safe for certain types of applications, some wools are made from melting plastics and can cause skin reactions in certain people.

♠Natural wool processing generally involves more steps, is labor-intensive, and requires seasonal and regional access to specific types of animals. IF there are issues within the animal population it affects the availability of wool. Artificial wool, is produced through a more industrial processes. Sometimes the industrial production involves slave or child labor or is unethical in some way. It's important to use fair trade or ethical sourced wool.

Environmental Impact: Natural wool can be more eco-friendly if sourced sustainably, while synthetic wool has a larger carbon footprint due to its dependence on petrochemicals as well as the conditions in which the products are manufactured. Most natural wools are created in smaller batches, whereas artificial wools can be created in large batches.

  Dyeing wool, whether natural or artificial, is an essential step to add color and enhance the aesthetic appeal of the final product. Dye can be made from natural elements such as fruit or vegetables or from unnatural elements such as synthetic red 40.

DYEING NATURAL WOOL

  Before dyeing, natural wool is usually washed and scoured to remove any dirt, grease, or lanolin. This helps the dye adhere better to the fibers. Natural wool can be dyed using a variety of dyes. Dyes are sourced from plants (like indigo or madder root), insects (like cochineal), or minerals (alum (potassium aluminum sulfate), iron salts (ferrous sulfate), and copper salts (copper sulfate). Synthetic dyes, which can create a wider range of colors and are more consistent in hue.

  Dye Bath Creation: For natural due, materials are typically boiled in water to extract the color. For synthetic dyes, a powder (created by the material chosen to create a color) is dissolved in hot water.

  Pre-treating the Wool: Sometimes, wool is treated with a mordant (a substance that helps fix the dye to the fibers) before the actual dyeing process begins. Mordants include alum or iron (which are also used to create a vibrant dye). This step is important, to ensure vibrant and lasting colors. In some books this is referred to as color 'fasting' in which the color is bound to the fabrics and resists fading when washed.

  Dyeing Process: clean wool is submerged in a dye bath. Cooked at a specific temperature for a specific period of time, depending on the type of dye and the desired color intensity. During this process, the wool is stirred to ensure the dye spreads to every fiber.

  Rinsing: Once the desired color is achieved, the wool is removed from the dye bath and rinsed in cool water until the water runs clear. This step removes any excess dye.

If you're hand spinning and dyeing it, use herbs and essential oils to really seal in the deal. If you are blocking it, wash it in the same herbs and essential oils. Let the person know the meaning behind the scent, so when they smell it they reinvigorate the spell.

❧Drying: Finally, the dyed wool is air-dried, away from direct sunlight to prevent fading.

Artificial Wool is generally prepared the same, however sometimes involve pre-treating which can make the wool easier to color.

❧Choosing the Dye: Artificial wool is usually dyed with synthetic dyes specifically formulated for the types of fibers used. These dyes are designed to bond effectively with synthetic materials.
❧3. Dye Bath Creation: Synthetic dyes are mixed with water to create a dye bath (similar to described above). The dye is chosen based on the fiber content of the wool for maximum effectiveness. Some artificial wools may require additional time to dye based on what ratio of natural fibers have been added.
❧ The Dyeing Process: The synthetic wool is submerged in a heated dye bath. Synthetic fibers require higher temperatures to properly absorb the dye. The wool is stirred to ensure even coloration.
❧Rinsing: Similar to natural wool, the wool is rinsed to remove excess dye until the water runs clear.
❧6. Drying: The dyed synthetic wool is dried either hanging out in natural air or using a dryer, depending on the care instructions and type of synthetic fiber.

Key Differences Between Dying Natural versus Artificial

🧹 Dye Types: Natural wool is dyed with both natural and synthetic dyes, while artificial wool primarily uses synthetic dyes.
🧹 Temperature: Synthetic wool requires higher temperatures during dyeing to achieve the desired colors, while natural wool processes at lower temperatures.
🧹 Mordants: Natural dyes often require a mordant process to fix the dye to the wool, which isn't necessary with synthetic wool.

CARING FOR WOOL GARMENTS

Whether made from natural or artificial fibers, all created products requires some attention to keep them looking great and prolong their lifespan.

1. Washing
   a.   Hand Washing: The best way to clean natural wool is by hand. Use cool or lukewarm water and a gentle wool detergent. Avoid hot water and harsh detergents, as they can cause shrinking or felting. The best detergent to use is Woolite as it is designed for knit/wool garments.
   b.   Machine Wash: If the garment is marked as machine washable, wash under a gentle cycle with cool/cold water. Always use a mesh laundry bag to protect the fibers.
2. Drying: After washing, gently press out excess water, using the flat of your hand or a light rolling pin, do not wring it out, as this can stretch the fibers. Lay the garment flat on a clean, dry towel to dry.
3. Storage: Store natural wool garments in a cool, dry place. Use breathable garment bags instead of plastic containers to prevent mildew. Consider adding cedar blocks or lavender sachets to deter moths.
4. Pilling: Natural wool can pill over time. Use a fabric shaver or a lint roller to remove any pills gently. Regular maintenance will keep your garment looking fresh.
5. Ironing: If you need to iron natural wool, use a cool setting and place a damp cloth between the iron and the fabric. This prevents scorching and helps to smooth out wrinkles.

CARING FOR ARTIFICIAL WOOL GARMENTS

1. Washing:
   a.   Machine Wash: Many artificial wool garments are machine washable. Just as with natural wool, its recommend to use the gentle cycle and mild detergent in cold/cool water.
   b.   Avoid Fabric Softeners: Fabric softeners can coat synthetic fibers and reduce their breathability, so it's best to skip them.
3. Drying: Machine drying is typically safe for artificial wool, if dried on low or medium heat to prevent any shrinking or damage. Alternatively, you can lay it flat to dry, which helps maintain its shape.

4. Storage: Like natural wool, artificial wool should be stored in a cool, dry place. Folding is recommended, to avoid stretching.
5. Pilling: Pilling can occur. Pilling is when the fibers create little pill type balls on the surface of the garment. To correct, use a fabric shaver to gently remove.
6. Ironing: If you need to iron synthetic wool, check the care label for the heat setting. If there are no specific instructions, use a low setting with no steam, as it may stretch or warp the fibers.

General Tips for Both Types Of Wool

- Read Care Labels: Always follow the care instructions on the garment's label, as they provide the best guidance.
- Avoid Heat: Both natural and artificial wool are sensitive to high temperatures, avoid hot water and high heat (when drying or ironing).
- Spot Cleaning: If there are small stains, try spot cleaning with a damp cloth and mild detergent before washing the entire garment. Some spot or stain removers are safe to use. The best for heavy stains are; Grandmas Stain Remover and Miss Messy Mouth.

Required Tools

- Yarn Different types and weights (e.g., worsted, bulky, sock)
- Stitch Markers: To mark pattern changes or sections.
- Row Counters: To keep track of the number of rows.
- Measuring Tape: For measuring gauge and finished dimensions.
- Darning or Tapestry Needle: For weaving in ends and seaming.
- Scissors: For cutting yarn.
- Yarn Bowl: To prevent yarn from tangling.
- Gauge Tool: To measure stitch and row gauge.

Knitting Tools

- Knitting Needles: Straight needles, Circular needles, Double-pointed needles (DPNs)
- Cable Needles: For holding stitches while crossing over in cable patterns.

CROCHET TOOLS

➳Crochet Hooks: Available in various sizes and materials (aluminum, plastic, steel).

SPINNING TOOLS

➳Spinning Wheel: The primary tool for spinning yarn from fiber.
➳Spindle: A simple tool for hand-spinning fibers (drop spindle or supported spindle).
➳Fiber: Raw material for spinning (wool, cotton, alpaca, etc.).
➳Niddy Noddy: For winding finished yarn into skeins.
➳Carders: For preparing fiber before spinning (hand carders or drum carders).
➳Diz: To pull fiber from a carder into a roving.
➳Yarn Winder: For winding skeins into balls or cakes.
➳Weigh Scale: To measure fiber quantities.

EMBROIDERY TOOLS

➳Embroidery Hoops: To hold fabric taut while working.
➳Embroidery Needles: Needles with larger eyes for embroidery threads
➳Embroidery Thread: like cotton floss, silk, or rayon.
➳Fabric: The base material to be embroidered (cotton, linen, etc.).

➳Water-Soluble Pen or Chalk: To mark designs on fabric for stitching.

➳Thimble: To protect fingers while stitching.

➳Needle Threader: To help thread needles easily.

CROSS-STITCH TOOLS

➤ Cross-Stitch Fabric: Usually Aida cloth or evenweave fabric.

➤ Embroidery Floss: Cotton threads specifically made for cross-stitch.

➤ Cross-Stitch Needles: Needles with a larger eye, suitable for embroidery floss.

➤ Embroidery Hoop: To keep the fabric taut during stitching.

➤ Scissors: For cutting threads.

➤ Fabric Marking Tools: Water-soluble pens or fabric markers for marking patterns.

➤ Pattern Chart: A printed or digital chart showing the design to be stitched.

➤ Needle Case: For organizing and storing needles.

➤ Thread Organizer: To keep embroidery threads organized and untangled.

FIBER ARTS IN BRIEF

Nalbinding is an ancient textile technique used to create fabric from yarn, predating knitting and crochet. The term "nalbinding" comes from the Old Norse word "nál," meaning "needle."

This technique involves using a single, blunt-ended needle to create interlocking loops, resulting in a fabric that is warm, durable, and often waterproof.

KEY FEATURES OF NALBINDING

Nalbinding is typically done with a long, blunt needle, which is made from wood, bone, or metal. Thicker wool is generally used to create a final product. The nalbinding technique involves making a series of interlocking loops, similar to a knit stitch, but without the use of multiple stitches or rows.

Each loop is formed directly from the previous loop, creating a dense fabric.

Unlike knitting or crochet, which can be unraveled easily, nalbinding creates a fabric which is more akin to traditional seams. This makes nalbinding projects quite durable and resistant to fraying.

Nalbinding dates back thousands of years and has been found in archaeological sites across Europe, the Middle East, and Egypt. It is considered one of the earliest methods of creating textiles, with evidence of nalbound items dating as far back as 6500 BCE.

There are several nalbinding stitch types, including:

    🦇 Coptic Stitch: A common stitch used to create fabric; it is one of the easiest to learn.

    🦇Oslo Stitch: A popular choice for making hats and socks due to its stretchy nature.

    🦇Mammoth Stitch: A technique suitable for thicker yarns and clothing.

Nalbinding was traditionally used to make socks, mittens, hats, and other garments, notably in cold climates, due to the warmth and durability of the fabric created. Nowadays, nalbinding is resurfacing as a craft and art form. Modern practitioners use it to create clothing, accessories, and decorative items. Often used in historical recreation.

Many textile enthusiasts and historians study nalbinding to understand historical garment construction techniques, which can shed light on ancient cultures and their textile practices. More recent finds have shown how durable the products are, having full pairs of socks preserved from as early as the bronze age.

COMPARISON TO OTHER TECHNIQUES

🦇Knitting: Unlike knitting, which uses two needles and allows for the creation of more flexible and open fabrics, nalbounding creates a denser and less elastic fabric. You will see this tight weave especially in socks, the dense weave creates a sturdy, tight, warm sock which would be vital in colder climates.

🦇Crochet: Nalbinding does not typically use a hook but employs a needle to create its fabric, leading to different textures and techniques compared to crochet.

KNITTING

Knitting likely originated in the Middle East around the 5th century CE, with the earliest known knitted items found in Egypt, dating back to the 11th century. By the 14th century, knitting was widespread throughout Europe. Hand-knit items became popular among both the wealthy and common people. Stockings, gloves, and caps were common knitted accessories.

It was a common holiday gift, in fact in some European cultures, industrious children were gifted 'woolen' items as Yule/Christmas gift. The tradition remains today in gifting; socks, scarfs, mittens and hats. The invention of the knitting machine by William Lee in the late 16th century revolutionized the industry. Today, knitting continues as a popular craft and is celebrated for its versatility in creating garments, accessories, and decorative items. There are now countless types of wool available to crafters, along with several classes to teach knitting to younger generations.

CROCHET

The exact origins of crochet are somewhat unclear, but it is thought to have developed in Europe during the 16th century, possibly evolving from other techniques like tambour or needle lace. By the 19th century, crochet gained popularity, particularly through the publication of patterns and books. It became associated with women's domestic crafts and was used to create intricate lace and decorative items. Often used to create accent pieces a lone, crochet evolved, becoming very popular through the 60s and 70s. Crochet grew to be a favorite for creating garments like vests, sweaters and pants, as well as blankets and keepsakes. Today, crochet is celebrated as both an art form and a practical craft, with a wide range of techniques and styles adapted for creating everything from fashion items to home decor.

SPINNING

Spinning is one of humanity's oldest textile technologies, dating back to around 20,000 years ago. The earliest spindles were made from wood, stone, or bone. Spinning technology evolved with the introduction of the spinning wheel in the Middle Ages. Today, both traditional hand-spinning techniques and industrial spinning methods are used, with renewed interest in artisanal and sustainable fiber arts.

Weaving

Weaving also has ancient roots, with evidence of woven textiles dating back to 5000 BCE. Early weavers used simple looms and natural fibers to create fabric. Often created on a standing loom or 'weighted' loom, although smaller 'tablet' looms have been well documented. Weaving techniques became more sophisticated, with advancements of the horizontal loom and the introduction of complex patterns and colors. By the Middle Ages, weaving had become a significant textile industry.

"Weaving magic could be used to help as well as harm. Often in riddles mail shirts are likened to magically woven protecting shirts. These shirts were called gørningstakkr or witch's shirts, and examples can be found in Eyrbyggja saga when Katla weaves a wound-proof shirt for her son Odd (ch. 18), in Vatnsdoela saga, where Ljót weaves one for her son Hrolleifr (ch. 19), as well as many other places in Norse literature. The motif is also well known in Finnish runos, where a mother weaves a magical shirt that is proof against the feared and deadly metal iron." The Viking Answer Lady

Embroidery

➳ Embroidery can be traced back to ancient civilizations, such as the Egyptians and Chinese, around 3000 BCE, where decorative stitching was used to embellish garments and textiles. While historically viewed as a pastime, activity, or hobby, intended just for women, embroidery has often been used as a form of biography. Women who were unable to access a formal education or, at times, writing implements, were often taught embroidery and utilized it as a means of documenting their lives by telling stories through their embroidery

Throughout history, different cultures have developed unique embroidery styles, incorporating local designs, materials, and techniques. By the Middle Ages, embroidery was a significant art form in Europe, often used to adorn religious garments and household linens.

CROSS-STITCH

Cross-stitch is a form of embroidery which likely originated in ancient Egypt, however it became more concrete and recognizable as an art form during the Middle Ages. It gained popularity in the 16th and 17th centuries, particularly in the form of samplers, which were used to teach young girls sewing and embroidery skills.

NALBINDING

Nalbinding is an ancient technique which predates knitting and crochet, dating back to around 6500 BCE in archaeological finds. It was practiced in various cultures, including the Northern Europeans and ancient Egyptians. Nalbinding was used to create warm garments, such as socks and hats. The technique involves using a single needle to make interlocking loops of yarn. Although this method is lesser-known than knitting or crochet, nalbinding has experienced a revival in recent years among textile enthusiasts and those interested in historical crafts and reenactment.

HOW FIBER ARTS PLAYED AN IMPORTANT ROLE IN EVERYDAY LIFE AND DEATH

Fiber arts were not just used to 'make things', there is (as mentioned) evidence of these crafts telling a story of the person's life, what they experienced (such as detailed tapestries), the skill they honed (elaborate stitch variants and detailed embellishments), the rites of passage they took part in (stitching swaddling cloth, funeral shrouds, bridal pieces, religious wear).

"Embroidery was destined to protect these specific and significant parts of the body. Most heavily embroidered – and the last item of Western European costume to disappear – was the coif: as can be seen in any village of Eastern Europe the headscarf and apron still linger as everyday wear, though they serve no practical purpose..." Folk Dance Footnotes[1]

---

[1] https://folkdancefootnotes.org/clothing/embroidery-decoration-or-magic/

The second most embroidered was the 'apron'. "The purpose of the ubiquitous apron of most European peasant costume, and particularly that of Eastern Europe, is symbolically protective and not practical. Varying in style with each village but normally heavily embroidered, intricately pleated or finely woven in striped patterning, it covered a dress or petticoat that almost always was deliberately left plain where the apron would be worn. It is the antithesis of an apron worn to protect precious clothing. Instead it protects the body." Folk Dance Footnotes[2]

Connection to Funeral Practices

Fiber Arts often play a role in funeral practices across many cultures, serving both practical and symbolic purposes:

➤Items such as shrouds, burial linens, and cloaks made from textiles hold cultural importance during burial rituals. In some traditions, specific colors or patterns are associated with mourning or honoring the deceased. Fiber Arts may be used to create memorial items, such as quilts or woven pieces which commemorate the life of a loved one. These textiles often carry personal stories or memories, acting as tangible connections to those who have passed away.

➤Participants in funerals may wear specific garments made from textile arts that symbolize mourning, respect, or cultural significance. The craftsmanship involved in creating these garments adds a personal touch to the ceremony.

"Mourning embroidery usually featured family members at the tomb of loved ones surrounded by weeping willows and angels. The monuments were personalized with the names and dates of the deceased. The weeping willow tree as a symbol of mourning reached the peak of its popularity in the 1820s. was reported to have asked to be buried under a weeping willow tree on St. Helena, the island of his final exile."

[2] https://folkdancefootnotes.org/clothing/embroidery-decoration-or-magic/

CONNECTION TO BIRTH PRACTICES

Fiber Arts are also intricately connected to birth practices and rituals:

➤Baby Garments: Many cultures emphasize the creation of handmade garments for newborns, such as blankets, onesies, or christening outfits, often made with love and care by family members. These items can symbolize the warmth and protection of the family. In certain rituals surrounding childbirth, items such as woven mats, blankets, or embroidered textiles may be used in birthing ceremonies or blessings. These items can convey cultural beliefs about fertility, protection, and community support for the new mother and child. Crafting items for a new baby can serve as a communal event, bringing family and friends together to celebrate the new life and support the parents. This fosters social bonding and shared cultural traditions.

"The belief that the fate of a child could be made, or altered, or irreparably harmed by this spinning has persisted, embodied in children's tales, such as the Märchen of Sleeping Beauty. This belief led to rituals performed by Swedish women, who in the seventh month of pregnancy drew blood from their finger with a sewing needle, and used it to mark a strip of wood with protective symbols. Then she spun three lengths of linen thread, which were dyed red, black, and one left white. The wooden strip was burned, and its ashes mixed with mead or beer. A burning twig from the fire was used to burn apart seven inch lengths from each of the linen threads, which were then boiled in salted water and left to dry in the forest on the limb of a tree for three days. These were then wrapped in clean linen and saved until the day of birth. The white cord was used to tie off the umbilical cord of the newborn. The red was tied around the baby's wrist as a protective amulet, sometimes strung with a bead to repel the evil eye. And the black , symbolic of death and ill-luck, was burned to ash and the ashes buried. Often the afterbirth was buried beneath the tree on which the linen threads had dried." The Viking Answer Lady

Connection to Rites of Passage

Fiber Arts often mark and celebrate various life transitions and rites of passage:

➤Handmade garments, stoles, or quilts are commonly used to commemorate graduation or coming-of-age ceremonies. These textiles symbolize the journey of growth and the support of the community.

➤Weddings: Fiber Arts are prominently featured in wedding ceremonies, where textiles like bridal gowns, veils, or table linens reflect personal and cultural meanings, as well as the collaborative effort of friends and family in creating or embellishing these items.

Many cultures have specific textiles associated with particular life stages, such as ceremonies marking adulthood, motherhood, or sacred obligations. The patterns and techniques used often carry traditional significance, expressing identity and heritage.

"Medieval embroidery was not only beautiful and much prized in its day, but it also had close links with other major medieval art forms such as illuminated manuscripts and tapestries, for there are frequent examples of the borrowing of motifs and designs among the various practitioners." Stitches in time: Medieval Embroidery in its Social Setting. M. Labarge

Knot Magic

Knot Magic and Magic-Cord Magic are techniques often used in crafting, especially in the context of macramé, knotting, and other textile arts. In pagan and heathen context, knot magic is often used when doing some kind of binding for protection or warding. It is often used in creating cording for garments or for rites of passage ceremonies.

TYPES OF KNOTS

There are numerous knots that can be used, each serving different purposes. Common knots include square knots, lark's head knots, and hitch knots. Each knot can add texture, strength, and visual interest to a project. Often knots are made in order, sometimes in specific counts (3 & 9) for magical workings.

DESIGN

Knot Magic involves the creative arrangement of knots to form intricate patterns and designs. By varying the type, size, and placement of knots, you can create a final piece which has specific intention and purpose. "Magical knots" can refer to both a specific technique for joining yarn in knitting or crocheting, and to the broader concept of knot magic, where knots are used as symbols or tools in spells and ritual.

The term 'magic circle' is generally used to denote a slip knot used to begin a crochet round, it allows for tension to be adjusted as the item is being created. Knotting for magic, is an old custom used to create 'tight bonds'. Prehistoric evidence shows us that our ancestors used knots thousands of years before they even invented the wheel. In a sense, knot-tying represents one of the oldest practices on this planet. It was used in many different ways, however we know at least in Northern magic (from the bronze-Viking age) knots were linked to otherworldly magic.

Intuitive Magic: is a spiritual or magical practice that emphasizes personal intuition and inner guidance as the primary tools for manifesting desires, understanding oneself, and connecting with the universe. It requires a practitioner to seek out more natural approaches, over following a strict practice rooted in academic or rule based practices.

~Considering the most powerful entities in mythology for the Norse were three women who 'spun fate' its not a stretch to see how they felt about thread magic. In the Saga of Eirik the Red, this encounter of a 'spinning woman' is recorded, you can clearly see the power she was thought to have;

"The web is not off the loom yet," Liv insisted. "What if you could unravel bits of it and reweave it? What if you could add a bit of lace or a new color? What if you could take something drab and make it beautiful? What if you could see the future and avoid trouble that is coming your way?"

"If you can do magic, then conjure up a sack of gold we can use to pay off the Knudsens," Eiric(k) shouted, his rage and helplessness driving him. He paused, calmed himself with an effort, then added, softly, "All I'm saying is that there are no miracles any more. The gods are not walking among us, pitching in now and then. We are not going to be saved by magic or anything else."

"Give up on magic if you want," Liv said, in a voice like spun steel. "If men give up sorcery, they still rule the world. They sit on the councils, they make the laws, they sail away and make their fortunes or die. Their lives go on much the same." She snatched up her distaff, the one she used to spin flax, and shook it in his face. "That is why magic is so often the province of women. It is the power we wield in the world, our ability to shape and change and control it. We would be foolish to give it up."

WHAT IS COLOR MAGIC?

Color magic is the practice of using color to enhance creativity, manifestation, and overall well-being. It is rooted in various cultural, spiritual, and artistic practices.

BASIC PRINCIPLES OF COLOR MAGIC

Different colors are believed to carry specific meanings and energies. For example:

~Red – Grounding energy, Strength, Passion, Courage, Lust, Charisma

~Orange – Creativity, success, justice, Opportunity, Ambition

~Yellow – Intelligence, Learning, Reason, Focus, Confidence, Memory, Joy

~Green – Nature, Healing, Money, Love, Fertility, Growth

~Blue – Communication, Traveling, expression, Forgiveness, Calm

~Purple – Influence, Psychic Abilities, Authority, Royal, Wisdom, Knowledge

~Brown – Home, Protection, Animals, Stability, Family

~Black – Banishing Negativity, Protection, binding, transmutation

~White – Spirituality, Peace, Higher Self, Purity

Colors are used to evoke certain feelings based on psychological principals, mythology and culture as well as available plant materials which were used for dyes but also had links to healing and other medicinal uses. Color magic does not have much historical context to draw from. It is based on intuitive magic and also developed by decades of shared knowledge passed down throughout many cultures.

Ritual Prayers

In pagan and heathen practices, prayer is a form of either vocally or silently evoking or petitioning the supernatural powers. These prayers serve various purposes, including invoking deities, expressing gratitude, seeking guidance, or marking significant events.

Key Characteristics of Ritual Prayers

Connection to Deities: In many pagan and heathen practices, we attempt to direct these petitions toward specific gods, goddesses, or spiritual beings. Practitioners may call upon these divine entities for assistance, blessings, or protection during rituals. When crafting, silently saying blessings over work is a form of a vocal 'casting' which words of protection, blessing and the like are spoken.

~Specific Structure: Ritual Prayers can vary in structure, generally they follow a similar form which includes:

  ♪ Invocation: Calling upon a deity or spirit. Generally this is when you would speak directly to the supernatural entity you wish to call.

Offerings: This is generally when you would pour out or gift a form of offering. Offerings generally come from mythological stories in which the gods or entities list out some of their favorite things. This could also be cultural or regional food commonly linked to the gods/entities who lived their, crafted items, purchased items, or any item you wish to freely give.

Affirmation: Expressing faith or devotion to the deity or spiritual principle being honored. This could also be replaced with a poem or specific worded offering which expresses a deep connection to the gods/entity invoked.

Ritual Prayers can be performed as part of communal gatherings, such as festivals, ceremonies, and rites of passage. They can be simple or elaborate depending on what you are trying to accomplish.

Twist me, twist me..Frigga,
Into your distaff,
Spin me, Spin me..Frigga,
Into your wheel,
Mould me, mould me.
.Frigga,
Into some wool,
Fix me, fix me..Frigga,
Into the web of wyrd.

-Larisa Hunter

Deities of Fiber Arts

Athena (Greek Mythology): goddess of wisdom and warfare, as well as weaving. She is often depicted with a spindle and is credited with teaching humans the art of weaving. She was depicted as a stately woman armed with a shield and spear, and wearing a long robe, crested helm, and the famed aigis--a snake-trimmed cape adorned with the monstrous visage of the Gorgon Medusa (Medusa).

Arachne (Greek Mythology): although not a goddess, Archane was a shepherd girl who is famously celebrated as a supreme weaver. Her cloth displays wonderful pictures and is loved by all who see it. In a contest against the goddess Athena, she was transformed into a spider, doomed to weave for all eternity.

Frigg (Norse Mythology): wife of Odin, Frigg is associated with domestic arts, including spinning and weaving. She is often linked to the Norns and spins the 'web of fate'. Depicted with a 'distaff', Frigga is said to 'spin the clouds', and in some stories, created flax, a fiber used in creating spun flax (linen)

Neith (Egyptian Mythology): As the Mistress of the Sea, she embodies the unbounded potential from which all life emanates, signifying the limitless depths of possibility inherent in the cosmic fabric. As she is connected with weaving, the symbol is sometimes suggested to be a shuttle.

Clotho (Greek Mythology): One of the Fates, Clotho is responsible for spinning the threads of fate. She was given credit for creating the alphabet, Clotho's decisions influenced both mortals and gods. Her role symbolized the interconnectedness of fate and the divine hierarchy within Greek mythology.

Lachesis (Greek Mythology): Another of the Fates, Lachesis measures the thread spun by Clotho, representing the length of life and destiny. She instructs the souls who are about to choose their next life, assign them lots, and presents them all of the kinds, human and animal, from which they may choose their next life.

Atropos (Greek Mythology): The third Fate, known as "the Inflexible One", Atropos cuts the threads of animals and humans, determining when and how their life ends.

Penelope (Greek Mythology): is married to the main character, the king of Ithaca, Odysseus (Ulysses in Roman mythology), and daughter of Icarus of Sparta and Periboea (or Polycaste). She only has one son with Odysseus, Telemachus, who was born just before Odysseus was called to fight in the Trojan War. She waits twenty years for Odysseus' return, during which time she devises various cunning strategies to delay marrying any of the 108 suitors (led by Antinous and including Agelaus, Amphinomus, Ctessippus, Demoptolemus, Elatus, Euryades, Eurymachus and Peisander). On Odysseus's return, disguised as an old beggar, he finds that Penelope has remained faithful. She has devised cunning tricks to delay the suitors, one of which is to pretend to be weaving a burial shroud for Odysseus's elderly father Laertes and claiming that she will choose a suitor when she has finished. Every night for three years, she undoes part of the shroud, until Melantho, a slave, discovers her chicanery and reveals it to the suitors.

Eir (Norse Mythology): A goddess of healing, Eir is often linked with spinning cloth in order to heal. Although not directly related to spinning or weaving, there are concepts within Nordic mythology which healing goddess would use magical linen or their own hair to bind wounds.

Folk Magic

"Granny magic" or "granny witchcraft" represents one flavor. Within this tradition, older women, called grannies, served as midwives, healers, and stewards of ancestral knowledge within their communities. These women knew the regenerative properties of certain native plants and provided medical care to those living in isolated areas, where residents were often distrustful of doctors. They concocted treatments for bladder and stomach problems, relief for burns and warts, and herbal methods for contraception and abortion. Catnip tea was commonly used to prevent hives, and sufferers placed sulfur in their shoes to ease flu. Between 1860 and 1980, Appalachian women held and used knowledge about herbal and home remedies that could be used at a time when many local governments restricted medical treatment to doctors. It was their unpaid labor that kept communities alive."

Refers to the practical application of magical practices, beliefs, and traditions which are rooted within a specific cultural heritage or region. It encompasses a wide range of rituals, spells, and remedies, which are typically passed down through generations, often integrated into the daily lives of practitioners.

Key Characteristics of Folk Magic

🜚 Cultural Roots: Folk Magic is deeply linked with the cultural and historical roots of the community from which it originates. It reflects local beliefs, customs, and practices, which combine elements of spirituality, superstition, and craftsmanship. Some of these have expanded or changed/evolved to be part of modern medicine as well as quackery.

Unlike more formalized religious/ceremonial magic, Folk Magic tends to be more practical, focusing on everyday problems and concerns. It uses elements which would have been readily available and often contain 'imported' material from contributing cultures which expanded the local folk magic into a more robust magic.

Common Practices in Folk Magic

Herbal Remedies: using herbs/plants/roots for healing and protection as well as curses and 'baneful' magic. It's important to use extreme caution with herbs/plants/roots as some are toxic.

Spells and Charms: written or verbal spell work is often used in folk magic. Charms can be created with natural materials or out of crafting a specific item with intention. Some spells may involve using specific items such as chalk to write out the spell.

Divination: Practitioners may employ various forms of divination to gain insight into their lives or the future. Tarot, spirit boards, runes, bones, random objects, planchets, dowsing rods, pendulums and the like are often employed.

Rituals and Celebrations: Seasonal festivals and celebrations, such as harvest festivals, solstice rituals, holy days,etc, play a significant role in Folk Magic. These rituals may include offerings, dances, or communal gatherings. Sometimes depending on the folk tradition, it may work around specific times of day/night or when certain celestial events are occurring.

Protective Measures: Many Folk Magic traditions emphasize protective practices, such as; amulets, talismans, or charms to ward off negative influences, misfortune, or illness. Some of these are simply the laying down of salt or brick dirt (thought to repel negative spirits) or laying 'iron nails' (to ward off evil).

Regional Variations

Folk Magic manifests differently across the globe, often reflecting local cultures and beliefs:

➤ Hoodoo: A form of African American folk magic primarily practiced within the Southern parts of the United States, blending African traditions with European influences. The practices are very misunderstood and often depicted as entirely baneful when in fact it is not either good or evil.

➤ Cunning Folk: In European traditions, these were individuals who practiced Folk Magic and served their communities in various roles, including healers, diviners, and wise folk. Its possible they may also have been midwives or people who knew the proper usage of herbs.

➤ Healing Practices: Many Indigenous cultures have their own forms of Folk Magic focused on healing, utilizing local plants, spiritual rituals, and ancestral beliefs. This also occasionally involves the use of 'sound' or vibration to help assist in healing.

➤ Appalachian Granny Magic: In the Appalachian region of the United States, there's a rich tradition of Folk Magic, often referred to as "Granny Magic," involving herbal remedies, charms, and community rituals.

Common Stitches

Embroidery Stitches

➤ Backstitch: Creates a solid line and is commonly used for outlining designs.

➤ Running Stitch: A simple stitch used for outlines or effects, forming dashed lines.

➤ Satin Stitch: A filling stitch that creates a smooth, glossy effect, ideal for solid shapes.

➤ French Knot: A small, raised knot created by wrapping thread around the needle before pulling it through.

➤ Chain Stitch: Forms a series of connected loops, useful for decorative outlining.

Counted Cross-Stitch

Counted cross-stitch is a specific form of embroidery where an X-shaped stitch is used to create images or patterns on a grid. This technique is called "counted" because the stitches are made on a pre-determined grid of fabric, usually Aida or evenweave, and the placement of each stitch is counted.

- Basic Cross-Stitch: The foundational X stitch created by making two diagonal stitches that cross each other.

- Half Cross-Stitch: A single diagonal stitch used to create shading or lessen the density of a design.

- Quarter Stitch: A small stitch that fills in missing corners of designs, providing additional detail.

Crochet Stitches

- The chain stitch

- The single crochet stitch

- The double crochet stitch

- The half double crochet stitch

- The treble crochet stitch

- The slip stitch

Knitting Stitches

- Garter Stitch

- Stockinette Stitch

- Stockinette Stitch st st

- Knit one, purl one (k1,p1) ribbing

- Knit two, purl two (k2, p2) ribbing

- Seed Stitch

- Double Stitch

Nalbinding Stitches

- Finnish Stitch (Family)

- Russian Stitch (Family)

- Turing Stitch (Family)

Stitches As the spell

Knit: The knit or garter stitch is the first stitch you learn. It's the foundation of most knitting stitches. Similar to the function of the white candle; it can be used for any kind of spell. A good stitch for beginners, this foundation can be used to make a variety of knitted items.

Purl: The purl stitch, is similar to the knit stitch, but when turned into a rib stitch or stockinette stitch, we change the intention of the stitch. Although it is a base stitch, it creates a new way to knit patterns. I find this stitch, a great way to do *reduction work*, to lighten a load or send something back, as both the rib stitch and stockinette stitch curl into each other which create an almost accordion-like effect.

Twist: A twist stitch creates a false cable. Like an enchantment or glamour, it creates illusion. Use it to boost the recipient's own abilities, but, be warned; this isn't a true cable, the person must have the abilities already, or others will see right through them.

Cable: Cables have a long history of being *protective stitches*. Fisherman's wives would create their own signature Aran style to identify their husbands if they were to wash ashore. Anything made with a cable should be used for luck, travel, or protection.

Lace: Lace is for beauty and love magic. These dainty garments invoke love and require a lot of passion to create.

There are so many stitches within knitting, its hard to add them all, the afore mentioned are just a taste of what you can use and what is possible to create. You can mix and match stitches to create multi-faceted spells. You can increase the potency of the knitted piece, by adding gemstones to your knitted piece. You could weave in herbs in order to imbue specific healing or beneficial herbal effects. From simple actions, like creating your own washes, which adds drops of oil to the cleansing process, to elaborate embellishments, its your spell and this is fibre art, the sky's the limit on what you can create.

Whether you use a whorl or a spinning wheel, enchanting the yarn you create can help boost or solidify any spell work you're doing. Remember to look at the animal or fibre association first, before you make a spell. For example, angora may not be the best for strength.

MAGICAL ASSOCIATIONS FOR EACH TYPE OF WOOL

Sheep: fertility, growth, success

Mohair: confidence, strength, protection

Angora: fertility, sex magick, energy, luck

Silk: strength, passion, love, beauty, hex craft

Linen: traditional magick, protection, prosperity

Cotton: catch all- use as a baseline when you don't know what to use

Alpaca: balance, stamina, return to sender

Athame

Items Needed: Black and red yarn

Instructions

Black and red yarn
With color a yarn cast on 6
stitches

Divide to work in the round
K1 m1*
K* re distribute stitches evenly
K1 m1*
K*
K1m1* 20 st
Knit 3 rounds
K1 k2tog* k1
K*
K 1 k2tog*
Inc in every stitch

Knit inc 1 at beginning and of
round and middle of the round
Knit for 4 inches
Work back and forth on one side
for 1 inch purling the ws row and
knitting the rs row break yarn
Then work back and forth on the
other side for 1 inch
Join back in the round
Knit 2 rounds
Switch to color b
K1 m1*
Knit
K1 m1* k1
Knit for 2 inches
Separate into two parts place half
of the athame on a stitch holder
there should be a defined front
and back, continue in stockinette
stitch)knit 1 row purl the next)
for 6 rows ending on a knit row.

42

Decrease rows
Row 1: k, k2tog knit to three stitches until end of row sl1 psso k1.
Row 2: knit
Repeat row 1 and 2 of the decrease until you have 3 stitches left

Go back to where you have the holes in the athame handle
Pick up 12 stitches and work in the round
Piece should measure approximately 0.5 of an inch
K1 m1 in each stitch of the round
k1 m1 in each stitch of the round
Knit 2 rounds
K2tog in each stitch of the round
K2tog in each stitch of the round

Take a darning needle and thread through the remaining stitches pull closed and tie off do the same for other side

Stuff the athame and stitch up the sides. Take read thread and stitch up the athame to make a middle part making it look more like a dagger weave in ends and you're finished.

Optional add selenite or black tourmaline to the wand for added oomph.

Sacred Rabbit Cardigan

Glossary

- BO: bind off
- CO: cast on
- k: knit
- k2tog: knit two together
- p: purl
- p2tog: purl two together
- rem: remaining
- RS: right side
- ssk: left -leaning decrease on knit side) slip,
slip, knit these 2 stitches together
- sl1, k1, psso: left leaning decrease on purl side) slip one, knit one, pass slipped stitch over
- St(s): stitches)
- WS: wrong side

Measurements: sizing for 36"/ 38"/40"/44"/48"/52" around chest

Gauge: 20 sts x 22 rows = 4" with 4.5 mm needles in stockinette

Needle Size: 4.5mm straight or circular needles (or size necessary to obtain gauge) & 3.5mm 24" circular needles (or one size smaller than main needles).

BACK

CO 90/95/100/110/120/130 in ash heather.

Ribbed edge:
   Work in k1/p1 for 16 rows.
Main back area:
   Work entire (left and right sides) chart for back.
   Continuing in black heather, on next row (RS), bind off 7/7/7/8/8/9 sts at beginning, and then continue to knit row to end.
   On next row (WS), bind off 7/7/7/8/8/9 sts at beginning, then continue to purl row to end. (Sts rem: 76/81/86/94/104/112.)
Decrease for armholes:
   On next knit row (RS), k1, ssk, k to last 3 sts, k2tog, k1. Purl next row (WS).
   Repeat decrease rows 8/9/9/10/12/12 more times. (Sts rem: 58/61/66/72/78/86.)

Decrease for armholes:

   On next knit row (RS), k1, ssk, k to last 3 sts, k2tog, k1. Purl next row (WS).
   Repeat decrease rows 8/9/9/10/12/12 more times. (Sts rem: 58/61/66/72/78/86.)
Continuing armhole shaping:
   Knit in stockinette until armhole is 8.5"/9"/9.5"/10"/10.5"/11" from BO row, and end with a WS row.
   Next row (RS): Bind off 6/7/8/9/10/12 sts.
   Next row (WS): Bind off 6/7/8/9/10/12 sts.
   Next row (RS): Bind off 6/6/7/8/10/11 sts.
   Next row (WS): Bind off 6/6/7/8/10/11 sts.
   Put rem 34/35/36/38/38/40 sts on stitch holder or thread onto a piece of scrap yarn (these are your neck sts).

Cardigan -Continued-

Continue neck and armhole shaping:

Work in stockinette until front measures 19.5"/21"/22.5"/23"/24"/25" from CO edge and end with RS row.

On next WS row, BO 7/7/7/8/8/9 sts for neck edge.

Continue working in stockinette, decreasing at neck edge every row for 4 rows, and then decreasing at neck edge every other row 3 more times.

For shoulder shaping, continue to work in stockinette until armhole measures 8.5"/9"/9.5"/10"/10.5"/11" from front left BO row.

On next RS row, BO 6/6/7/8/10/11 sts for shoulder edge.
   (WS) Purl 1 row.
   (RS) BO rem sts (9/10/13/14/15/17).

Front Right

CO 45/47/50/55/60/65 sts in ash heather.

Ribbed edge: Ribbed edge: Work in k1/p1 for 16 rows.

Jackalope front right: Work right portion of chart for front right.

Continue front right area:

Continuing in black heather, on next WS row, BO 7/7/7/8/8/9 sts. (Sts rem: 38/40/43/47/52/56).
   Knit next row.

Decrease for armholes:
   Decrease rows: On WS row, p1, p2tog, p to end.
Knit RS rows.
   Repeat decrease rows 8/9/9/10/12/12 more times.
Continue neck and armhole shaping:
   Work in stockinette until front measures 19.5"/21"/22.5"/23"/24"/25" from CO edge and end with WS row.
   On next RS row, BO 7/7/7/8/8/9 sts for neck edge.
   Continue working in stockinette, decreasing at neck edge every row for 4 rows, and then decreasing at neck edge every other row 3 more times.
   For shoulder shaping, continue to work in stockinette until armhole measures 8.5"/9"/9.5"/10"/10.5"/11".

Cardigan -Continued-

On next WS row, BO 6/7/8/9/10/12 sts for shoulder edge.

(RS) Knit 1 row.

(WS) BO rem sts (9/10/13/14/15/17).

Neck band

Sew both shoulder seams. (I like to use mattress stitch for seaming.)

With RS facing you and beginning at right neckline with ash heather, use the 4.5 mm circular needle to pick up and knit the sts on the right neckline, the sts on the st holder, and around the left neckline.

Work in k1/p1 rib for 30 rows (first row will be a WS row).

BO.

Buttonhole band (right side)

Place evenly spaced markers on sweater to mark locations for button holes.

With RS facing you and starting at bottom right with ash heather, use the 3.5 mm circular needle to pick up sts along front right and up to top of neck band.

Work in k1/p1 for 3 rows.

On row 4, work in ribbed pattern until you reach marker for button. At this point, BO 2 sts (based on 3/4" buttons — you can BO more or less sts as necessary to fit your button). Repeat the 2-stitch BO at remaining button markers.

On row 5, working in ribbed pattern, work until you reach first bound off sts, and then CO 2 sts for other side of the buttonhole. Repeat at all bound off sts on button band.

Work 3 more rows in ribbed pattern.

BO all stitches.

If desired, finish by sewing or crocheting around buttonholes to reinforce them.

Button band (left side)

With the 3.5 mm circular needle, RS facing you, and starting at top left in ash heather, pick up an equal number of sts as on the buttonhole band.

Work 8 rows of ribbing (k1/p1).

(RS) BO.

Sleeves (make 2)

Ribbing:

With 4.5 mm needle, CO 42/46/50/54/58/62 sts in ash heather.

K1/p1 for 16 rows, ending with a WS row.

Shaping:

With black heather, K1, kfb, knit to last 3 sts, kfb, k1.

Knit 8 rows

Repeat the last two rows 8 more times, and then repeat first row once more (sts after increases: 62/66/70/74/78/82).

Knit until length of sleeve reaches: 18/18.5/19/19.5/19.5/20/20.5".

BO 6/6/6/7/7/8 at beginning of next two rows.

Cardigan -Continued-

In same manner as previous decrease method (which was k1, ssk, knit to last 3 sts, k2tog, k1), continue to decrease by 2 sts on every RS row 7/8/7/8/10/10 times .

Decrease every row at each end until 18/20/20/22/24/26 sts remain (on RS rows, follow decrease convention above, and on WS rows, p1, sl1, k1, psso, purl to last 3 sts, p2tog, p1).

BO rem sts.

Assembly

Seam sides of cardigan.

Pin sleeves in place and seam (find centre of sleeve by folding top of sleeve cap in half).

Sew on buttons and weave in all loose ends.

Wash gently and block.

Cardigan -Continued-

Right Side   Left Side

Right Side   Left Side

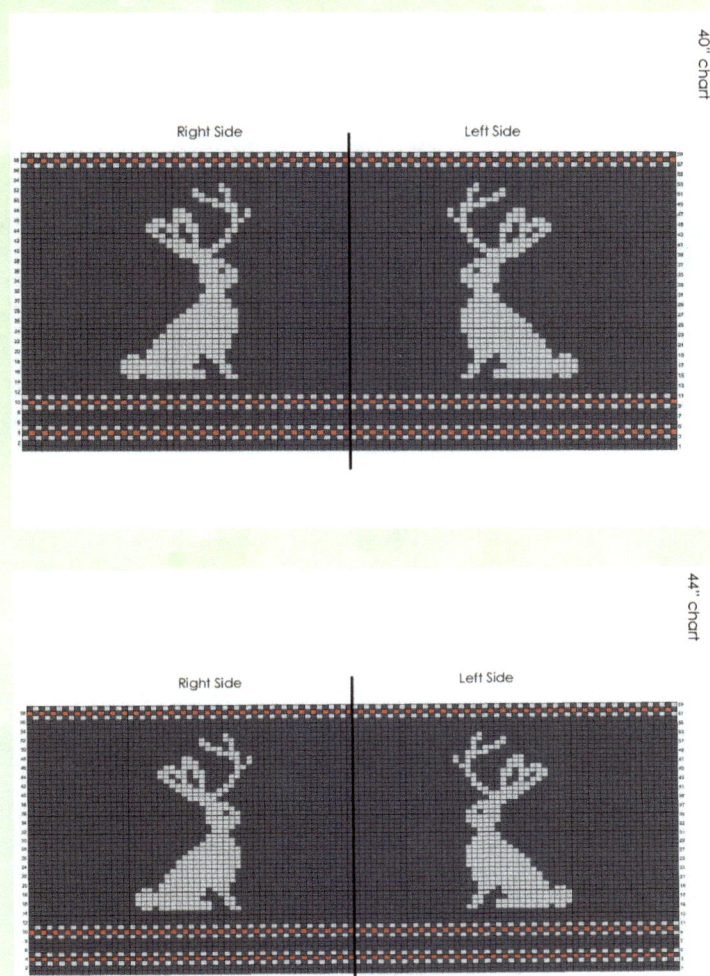

Right Side   Left Side

Right Side   Left Side

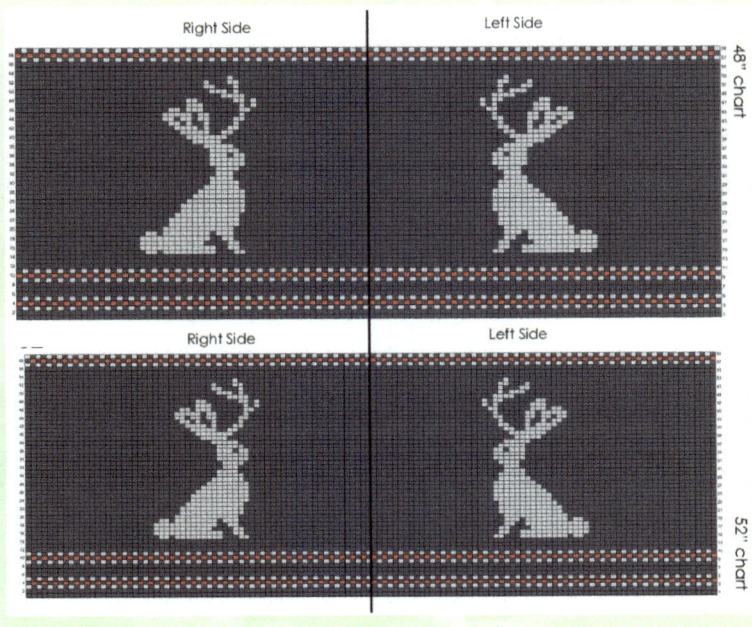

Queen Witch Wrap

Needles....4mm US 6 and a 6mm US 10 for casting off.
Stitch markers if you wish to keep track of large amounts of needles.
I have used Honey Girl Farms yarns in the following shades
1 x Danaerys Targaryen 100g on deluxe sock 400m/437 yrds
1 x Indi Blue 100g on deluxe sock 400m/437 yrds
The overall meterage used was approx. 800m of 4ply/fingering weight yarn

Abbreviations

K...Knit
P...Purl.
Kfb.. knit the next stitch and whilst its still on the needle knit into the back of it to create
a new stitch.
Kfbf.. knit the next stitch and whilst still on the needle knit into the back and then again
into the front to create two extra stitches.
K2tg.. knit the next 2 stitches together
Yo.. wrap the yarn over the needle.
Slp1pw.. slip the stitch onto the right hand needle without working it in a purl wise direction
Co.. Cast off
Gauge... isn't necessary with this pattern.
You will see there is no stitch count for the pattern, the first skein is worked until its finished with an even number of stitches on the needles, and the lace skein section is also worked just having an even number of stitches on the rows.

When I cast off I had 488 stitches, to give you an idea what you will be working with, but slightly more or slightly less will make no difference to the pattern providing the number is even.

You may like to add some stitch markers as you work if you are someone who likes to count the stitches each row, but its not essential for the pattern.

Cast On Tab
Cast on 3 stitches using the solid color or first skein
Work 5 rows by knitting all stitches
Turn the work 90 deg and pick up 3 stitches
Turn the work 90 deg again and pick up 3 stitches evenly spaced along the cast on
edge.
There are now 9 sts and you need to work one row knitting all the stitches

Set Up Row
K1, kfb, yo, k2, kfb, k2, yo, kfb, k1 (you now have an even number of stitches to start)
Main pattern
Row 1. K1, kfb, yo, (k1,p1) repeat bracket instruction to last 2 sts, yo, kfb, k1
Row 2. K1, kfbf, purl to the last 2 sts, kfbf, k1
Repeat these 2 rows to the end of the first skein finishing on a row 2, on that row knit the stitches across rather than purl them.

MAIN PATTERN

Row 1. K1, kfb, yo, (k1,p1) repeat bracket instruction to last 2 sts, yo, kfb, k1
Row 2. K1, kfbf, purl to the last 2 sts, kfbf, k1
Repeat these 2 rows to the end of the first skein finishing on a row 2, on that row knit the stitches across rather than purl them.

Witch Wrap-Continued-

Change to 2nd skein and work the following rows....
Row 1. K1, kfb, yo, knit to the last 2 sts, yo, kfb, k1
Row 2. K1, kfbf, (k2tg, yo) repeat the bracket to last 2 sts, kfbf, k1
Row 3. K1, kfb, purl to last 2 sts, kfb, k1
Row 4. K1, kfbf, purl to last 2 sts, kfbf, k1
Row 5. K1, kfb, (k2tg, yo) repeat bracket to last 2 sts, kfb, k1
Row 6. K1, kfbf, purl to last 2 sts, kfbf, k1
Row 7. K1, kfb, yo, knit to last 2 sts, yo, kfb, k1
Row 8. K1, kfbf, purl to last 2 sts, kfbf, k1
Row 9. K1, kfb, yo, k1, (yo, slp1pw, k1, pass the yo over the slipped and knit stitch) repeat the bracket to last 3 sts, k1, yo, kfb, k1
Row 10. K1, kfbf, purl to the last 2 sts, kfbf, k1
Row 11. K1, kfb, yo, k1, (yo, slp1pw, k1, pass the yo over the slipped and knit stitch)
repeat the bracket to last 3 sts, k1, yo, kfb, k1
Row 12. K1, kfbf, purl to the last 2 sts, kfbf, k1
Row 13. K1, kfb, (k2tg, yo) repeat to last 2 sts, kfb, k1
Row 14. K1, kfbf, purl to the last 2 sts, kfbf, k1
Row 15. K1, kfb, (k2g, yo) repeat to last 2 sts, kfb, k1
Row 16. K1, kfbf, purl to the last 2 sts, kfbf, k1
Row 17. K1, kfb, (k2tg, yo) repeat to last 2 sts, kfb, k1
Row 18. K1, kfbf, k1, (k2tg, yo) repeat to last 3 sts, k1, kfbf, k1
Row 19. K1, kfb, k1, (k2tg, yo) repeat to last 3 sts, k1, kfb, k1
Row 20. K1, kfbf, (yo, k2tg) repeat to last 2 sts, kfbf, k1
Row 21. K1, kfb, k1, (k2tg, yo) repeat to last 3 sts, k1, kfb, k1
Row 22. K1, kfbf, (yo, k2tg) repeat to last 2 sts, kfbf, k1
Row 23. K1, kfb, yo, k1, (k2tg, yo) repeat to last 3 sts, k1, yo, kfb, k1
Row 24. K1, kfbf, k1, (yo, k2tg) repeat to last 3 sts, k1, kfbf, k1
Row 25. K1, kfb, (k2tg, yo) repeat to last 2 sts, kfb, k1
Row 26. K1, kfbf, k1, (yo, k2tg) repeat to last 3 sts, k1, kfbf, k1

Row 27. K1, kfb, yo, knit to last 2 sts, yo, kfb, k1
Row 28. K1, kfbf, knit to last 2 sts, kfbf, k1
Row 29. K1, kfb, yo, knit to the last 2 sts, yo, kfb, k1
Row 30. K1, kfbf, purl to last 2 sts, kfbf, k1
Row 31. K1, kfb, yo, k1, (yo, slp1pw, k1, pass the yo over the slipped and knit stitch)
repeat the bracket to last 3 sts, k1, yo, kfb, k1
Row 32. K1, kfbf, k1, (yo, k2tg) repeat to last 3 sts, k1, kfbf, k1
Row 33. K1, kfb, yo, knit to the last 2 sts, yo, kfb, k1
Change to 6mm needle and cast off all stitches working a 3 stitch picot on the first and
last stitch.
Sew in the ends and block into crescent shape.

Finished dimensions.... Approx. 160cm wide and 40cm deep after blocking.

Evil eye pouch

Color Legend

A-black
B-blue
C-white

Items Needed: Size 5 mm
needles

Cast on 3 stitches on circular
needles separate
Round 1 k1 m1*
Re distribute stitches
Round 2 k1 m1*
Round 3 knit
Round 4 k1 m1
Round 5 knit
Round 6 k2 m1*
knit
Knit 3 m1
Knit
Knit 4 m1
Knit
Knit 5 m1
Knit

Change to color b
K6 m1*
Knit
K7 m1*
Knit
Knit 8 m1*
Knit
Knit 9 m1*
Knit
Knit 10 m1*
Knit

Knit 11 m1*
Knit
Change to color c
Knit 12 m1*
Knit
Knit 13 m1*
Knit
Knit 14 m1*
Knit
Knit 15 m1*
Knit
Knit 16 m1*
Knit
Knit 17 m1*
Knit
Knit 18 m1*
Knit
Stretchy bind off (knit 2 knit both together knit [...] both together repeat)

The evil eye pouch was one of my first ever knitting patterns. I originally made one so small I could wear it around my neck using it to hold crystals or other trinkets. I've since lost the original and made this one slightly bigger to hold crystals or trinkets in your purse/ bag. The evil eye is a protection symbol from the middle east but has since spread around the world as a way to ward off evil. The colors represent different areas of protection. Each color has a different area in which you wish to focus the evil eye's power. I made mine in the traditional black white and blue colors but really with a little bit of research any color can be used. Remember to use your own personal gnosis when using the colors. Yes these are ancient symbols but if you feel red is protection and blue is healing, who's to tell you you are wrong?

Repeat pattern for second side

-If the eye seems triangular then fold inwards the black and tie off until it lies flat and appears round.

Take a 2mm crochet hook and slip stitch with color b around the two sides pressed together right sides out keeping a wide enough gap to fit a crystal

Single crochet around the gap to make an opening single crochet 3-4 rounds to tidy it up and make it look pouch like. Depending on if you want a draw string add more rows

Alternatively before joining the halves you can block the eye to make it lay flatter. However I opted not to as I used acrylic yarn and don't have a steamer

Poppet

If you want to make this like a traditional Ukrainian motanka for go metal needles and use wooden ones and rip the yarn as metal should never pierce the thread of the motanka.

Suggested: For the poppet using 4.5 mm needles and light worsted or DK yarn in corresponding color to what you want to use the poppet for I used purple for compassion. (Any weight and size needles work for this project) The fibre is only important if you choose to leave this out in nature if you're going to leave this outside or bury it please use undyed organic yarn. Such as alpaca, single spun wool, or organic non mercerized cotton.

Instructions

Cast on 4 stitches
Row 1:knit
Row 2: k1 m1 m1 k1
Row 3:knit
Row 4:k1 m1 knit to the last 2 stitches left m1 k1
Row 5: knit
Row 6: k1 m1 knit till 2 stitches left m1 k1
Row 7-10: knit
Row 11: k1 k2tog knit to last 3 stitches s1psso knit
Row 12: knit
Row 13: k1 k2tog knit to last 3 stitches s1psso knit
Row14: knit
Row 15: k1 k2tog knit to last 3 stitches s1psso knit
Row 16: knit
Row 17:knit

The poppet is a doll used for sympathetic magic meaning you use the doll to imbue the recipient with the magic. Motanka's are very much the same. Motanka's are specific to Ukrainian culture but you can find a variety of doll-like figures in many cultures used to rid the person of the evil eye, sickness, or to promote healing. I made mine to bring in more compassion. Since becoming pregnant I've become hyper vigilant and wary of my fellow person. I want to invoke more compassion and understanding into my life. So a poppet to remind me to be more compassionate that works alongside me was the perfect response. As a reminder all these projects can be amped up by blessing or imbuing them with your own magical charms, incantations, or spells. The only limit is your imagination.

Row 18: k1 *m1 I! Each stitch until the last stitch* k1
Row 19: knit
Row 20: k1 *m1 in every stitch until the last stitch* k1
Now knit the first 4 place on stitch holder
Knit then place the last 4 on a stitch holder do not knit these stitches at this time

With 7 stitches left on the needle knit
Knit until the piece is the length you want I want a fairly small poppet so I'll do 5 rows do more depending on weight of wool and size of needles

Legs

Next work 4 stitches and place on stitch holder
Then m1 and knit to the end this is the beginning of the leg
Work in the knit stitch for 5 rows
K1 k2tog k1
K1 k2tog
K2tog
Bind off
Repeat for other leg picking up the stitches on the stitch holder

Poppet Continued

Arms:
pick up stitches on either arm and knit 3 rows
K1 k2tog k1
K1 k2tog
K2 tog bind off
Continue for second arm

You'll make another poppet exactly the same as the first.
Sew the two sides together and fill with herbs, stones, or
cotton in the corresponding elements you wish to achieve

Travel Alter/shrine

The shrine/ altar is a place to focus your magical workings. I made one that could in your purse or bag. Something easy to take with you if you're still in the broom closet or a traveling witch. I made the patterns in my book really plain so your imagination can run free and really make these your own. I got the idea from catholic pocket shrines, where they have pictures and prayers sewn into them. What a neat way to honor your patron saint, deity, or genus loci. Add as much or as little decoration as you wish. I used wool so it's not flammable. But you can use any fibre you wish so long as you're not burning candles or incense on it.

With chunky yarn and 8mm needles cast on 24 stitches.

Knit until 15 inches long

Once 15 inches knit 1 k2tog, knit till last 3 stitches s1k1 psso, knit final stitch

Continue until 5 stitches left.
K1 k3tog
K2tog
Bind off

Travel Alter/shrine Continued

Now fold the pattern into 3 equal parts the top and bottom should fold in and overlap

Starting at the crease pick up 20 stitches on either the left or right side following the finished edge.

Next knit these stitches until the piece reaches just to the other side of the width of the piece bind off

Do the same for the opposite side
Decorate to your heart's content. Sew on photos, lace, embroidery, anything to help you remember this is your practice and mini altar

Wand

Wands are a quintessential witches tool. When you think witch you think wand. I decided to make two, one for people who like a handle and one that is more typical of a witches wand. I wanted to make sure those with arthritis had a comfortable wand too. Since everyone has different bodily capabilities.

When you make your wand think of what types of magic you wish to do with said wand. You can add herbs, crystals, embellishments, or rigidity (floral wire, wire, a stick) to the knitted wand to achieve your desired outcome.

The wand is a conduit of your power. You don't need a wand to draw power, you have your body, but for those who like a bit of flourish and mental clarity on where they're directing that power a wand is an amazing tool. I like wands and knew I had to knit my own.

Co 12 stitches

Round 1: stitches evenly (6 per needle circular needle with magic loop) (3 per needle for dbl points) knit for the round
Round 2: continue knitting until the piece measures 13 inches.

Sew up the bottom and stuff with polyfill cotton or wool include any herbs or crystals /charms your heart desires then sew up the end when it is filled to your liking.

Changeling Prevention Hat

Before crocheting a hat, you need to measure the circumference of the head. If this is not possible, then use the table.

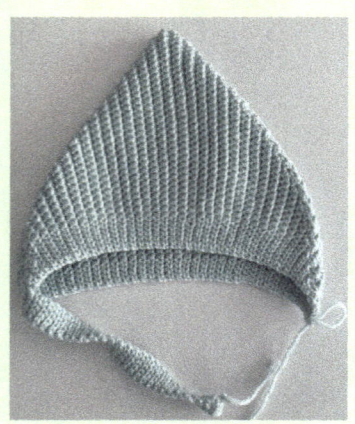

AGE	Head circumference X		Approx Bonnet width A		Approx Bonnet length B	
	cm	inches	cm	inches	cm	inches
0-3 months	38	15,7	14,5	5,7	14	5,5
3-6 months	42	16,5	15,5	6,1	16	6,3
6-12 months	46	18,1	17,0	6,7	17	6,7
1-2 year	48	18,9	17,5	6,9	17	6,7
2-3 year	50	19,7	18,5	7,3	18	7,1
3-5 years	52	20,5	19,0	7,5	20	7,9

Abbreviation Description

BLO back loop only
ch chain stitch
FLO front loop only
RS right side
sc single crochet
ss slip stitch
WS wrong side
inc3 increase – work 3 single crochet stitches in one stitch
sc3tog single crochet 3 stitches together
(...) number of sts in total
rep (...) *N repeat in brackets N times
rep repeat

Step 1. Lace (similar for all sizes)
Chain 4+1, turn [fig 1]
Row 1: 4 ss, ch 1, turn.
Rows 2-50: repeat Row 1 [fig 2]. Don't cut the yarn!

Step 2. Mane part (for size 3-6 months baby)
Row 1: ch1, crochet in the 2nd loop from the hook inc3 (put the marker on the 2nd sc [fig 3]), 4 ss, ch 1, turn.

Row 2: 4 ss, 1 sc, inc3, 1 ss, ch 1, turn.
Row 3: 2 ss, inc3, 2 sc, 4 ss, ch 1, turn
Row 4: 4 ss, 3 sc, inc3, 3 ss, ch 1, turn.
Row 5: 4 ss, inc3, 4 sc, 4 ss, ch 1, turn.
Row 6: 4 ss, 5 sc, inc3, 5 ss, ch 1, turn.
Row 16: 4 ss, 15 sc, inc3, 9 sc, 6 ss, ch 1, turn.
Row 17: 6 ss, 10 sc, inc3, 16 sc, 4 ss, ch 1, turn.
Row 18: 4 ss, 17 sc, inc3, 11 sc, 6 ss, ch 1, turn.
Row 19: 6 ss, 12 sc, inc3, 18 sc, 4 ss, ch 1, turn.
Row 20: 4 ss, 19 sc, inc3, 13 sc, 6 ss, ch 1, turn.
Row 21: 6 ss, 14 sc, inc3, 20 sc, 4 ss, ch 1, turn.
Row 22: 4 ss, 21 sc, inc3, 15 sc, 6 ss, ch 1, turn.
Row 23: 6 ss, 16 sc, inc3, 22 sc, 4 ss, ch 1, turn.
Row 24: 4 ss, 23 sc, inc3, 17 sc, 6 ss, ch 1, turn.
Row 25: 6 ss, 18 sc, inc3, 24 sc, 4 ss, ch 1, turn.
Row 26: 4 ss, 25 sc, inc3, 19 sc, 6 ss, ch 1, turn.
Row 27: 6 ss, 20 sc, inc3, 26 sc, 4 ss, ch 1, turn.
Row 28: 4 ss, 27 sc, inc3, 21 sc, 6 ss, ch 1, turn.
Row 29: 6 ss, 22 sc, inc3, 28 sc, 4 ss, ch 1, turn.
Row 30: 4 ss, 29 sc, inc3, 23 sc, 6 ss, ch 1, turn.
Row 31: 6 ss, 24 sc, inc3, 30 sc, 4 ss, ch 1, turn.
Row 32: 4 ss, 31 sc, inc3, 25 sc, 6 ss, ch 1, turn.
Row 33: 6 ss, 26 sc, inc3, 32 sc, 4 ss, ch 1, turn.
Row 34: 4 ss, 33 sc, inc3, 27 sc, 6 ss, ch 1, turn.
Row 35: 6 ss, 28 sc, inc3, 34 sc, 4 ss, ch 1, turn.
Row 36: 4 ss, 35 sc, inc3, 29 sc, 6 ss, ch 1, turn.
Row 37: 6 ss, 30 sc, inc3, 36 sc, 4 ss, ch 1, turn

Measure the width and height of the hat. Compare with the table (page 3).
To get a large size, crochet more rows with increases, similar to the pattern.

Changeling Prevention Hat Continued

Then crochet 2 rows without increments, simply transferring the marker.
Row 38: 4 ss, 37+1+31 sc, 6 ss, ch 1, turn.
Row 39: 6 ss, 31+1+37 sc, 4 ss, ch 1, turn.
Then crochet the second half of the hat – rows with decrease
- sc3tog –
single crochet 3 stitches together

Row 40: 4 ss, 36 sc, sc3tog, 30 sc, 6 ss, ch 1, turn.
Row 41: 6 ss, 29 sc, sc3tog, 35 sc, 4 ss, ch 1, turn.
Row 42: 4 ss, 34 sc, sc3tog, 28 sc, 6 ss, ch 1, turn.
Row 43: 6 ss, 27 sc, sc3tog, 33 sc, 4 ss, ch 1, turn.
Row 44: 4 ss, 32 sc, sc3tog, 26 sc, 6 ss, ch 1, turn.
Row 45: 6 ss, 25 sc, sc3tog, 31 sc, 4 ss, ch 1, turn.
Row 46: 4 ss, 30 sc, sc3tog, 24 sc, 6 ss, ch 1, turn.
Row 47: 6 ss, 23 sc, sc3tog, 29 sc, 4 ss, ch 1, turn.
Row 48: 4 ss, 28 sc, sc3tog, 22 sc, 6 ss, ch 1, turn.
Row 49: 6 ss, 21 sc, sc3tog, 27 sc, 4 ss, ch 1, turn.
Row 50: 4 ss, 26 sc, sc3tog, 20 sc, 6 ss, ch 1, turn.
Row 51: 6 ss, 19 sc, sc3tog, 25 sc, 4 ss, ch 1, turn.
Row 52: 4 ss, 24 sc, sc3tog, 18 sc, 6 ss, ch 1, turn.
Row 53: 6 ss, 17 sc, sc3tog, 23 sc, 4 ss, ch 1, turn.
Row 54: 4 ss, 22 sc, sc3tog, 16 sc, 6 ss, ch 1, turn.
Row 55: 6 ss, 15 sc, sc3tog, 21 sc, 4 ss, ch 1, turn.
Row 56: 4 ss, 20 sc, sc3tog, 14 sc, 6 ss, ch 1, turn.
Row 57: 6 ss, 13 sc, sc3tog, 19 sc, 4 ss, ch 1, turn.
Row 58: 4 ss, 18 sc, sc3tog, 12 sc, 6 ss, ch 1, turn.
Row 59: 6 ss, 11 sc, sc3tog, 17 sc, 4 ss, ch 1, turn.
Row 60: 4 ss, 16 sc, sc3tog, 10 sc, 6 ss, ch 1, turn.
Row 61: 6 ss, 9 sc, sc3tog, 15 sc, 4 ss, ch 1, turn.
Row 62: 4 ss, 14 sc, sc3tog, 8 sc, 6 ss, ch 1, turn.
Row 63: 6 ss, 7 sc, sc3tog, 13 sc, 4 ss, ch 1, turn
Row 64: 4 ss, 12 sc, sc3tog, 6 sc, 6 ss, ch 1, turn.
Row 65: 6 ss, 5 sc, sc3tog, 11 sc, 4 ss, ch 1, turn.
Row 66: 4 ss, 10 sc, sc3tog, 4 sc, 6 ss, ch 1, turn.
Row 67: 6 ss, 3 sc, sc3tog, 9 sc, 4 ss, ch 1, turn

Row 68: 4 ss, 8 sc, sc3tog, 2 sc, 6 ss, ch 1, turn.

Row 69: 6 ss, 1 sc, sc3tog, 7 sc, 4 ss, ch 1, turn.
Row 70: 4 ss, 6 sc, sc3tog, 6 ss, ch 1, turn.
Row 71: 5 ss, sc3tog, 5 sc, 4 ss, ch 1, turn
Row 72: 4 ss, 4 sc, sc3tog, 4 ss, ch 1, turn.
Row 73: 3 ss, sc3tog, 3 sc, 4 ss, ch 1, turn.
Row 74: 4 ss, 2 sc, sc3tog, 2 ss, ch 1, turn.
Row 75: 1 ss, sc3tog, 1 sc, 4 ss, ch 1, turn.
Row 75: 4 ss, sc3tog, ch 1, turn.
Row 76: 4 ss, ch 1, turn

Step 3. Lace (similar for all sizes)
Row 76: 4 ss, ch 1, turn.
Rows 77-127: repeat Row 76.
Cut the yarn! Hide the ends.

Suggested Embroidered Runes to protect an infant from any negative harm.

Tomte or Gnome

Yarn: DK skein 100% Acrylic in 6 colors
      YARN A - Body/Arms = *Dark Green (25g)*
      YARN B - Hat = *Light Green (25g)*
      YARN C - Nose/Hands = *Beige (8 meters)*
      YARN D - Beard/Flower = *White (+- 3m for beard + 1m for flower)*
      YARN E - Flowers = *Yellow (2-3m for each flower)*
      YARN F - Flower Center = *Black (1m each flower center)*

Hook: 3.0 mm

Extras: Fiberfill Stuffing (25g) & Cardboard for the Base (4.2cm)

Notions: Measuring Tape, Yarn Needle, Scissors, Stitch Markers

Finished Gnome size is approx. 8.5 inches / 22cm high

Meterage and grams given for yarn is an approximate, you might use fewer or more depending on your working tension.

Abbreviations

ch sc sl st st/s MR BLO
Chain
Single Crochet
Slip Stitch
Stitch / Stitches
Magic Ring
Work Back Loops Only

Arms Make 2

Start with a Yarn Color
C
Round 1 : MR, sc 6 (6)
Round 2: *sc inc, sc*
Rep 3 (9)
Round 3 - 4: sc 9 (9)
Change to Yarn Color A
Round 5 - 12: sc 9 (9), sl
st
Cut a long tail

Nose-Make 1

Use Yarn color C
Round 1 : MR, sc 6 (6)
Round 2: *sc inc, sc*
Rep 3 (9)
Round 3: *sc inc, sc 2*
Rep 3 (12)
Round 4 - 5: sc 12 (12),
sl st

Cut a long tail.
Body-Make 1

Round 1 : MR, sc 6 (6)
Round 2: sc inc in each
st (12)
Round 3: *sc inc, sc*
Rep 6 (18)

Round 4: *sc inc, sc 2*
Rep 6 (24)
Round 5: *sc inc, sc 3*
Rep 6 (30)

Measure the size and
cut a circular piece from
your cardboard

Round 6: BLO *sc inc,
sc 4* Rep 6 (36)
Round 7: *sc inc, sc 5*
Rep 6 (42)
Round 8: sc 42 (42)

Round 9: *sc inc, sc 6*
Rep 6 (48)
Round 10 - 21: sc 48
(48)

Place the cardboard at
the bottom of your
gnome body and start
adding stuffing.

sl st to secure your yarn
and add a stitch marker
in stitch 12, 24 and 36.

We are going to attach
the nose , arms and add
the beard next.

Tomte or Gnome Continued

Assembly

ATTACH THE ARMS

First, using your yarn tail and yarn needle, sew through the FLO of your stitches to close the arms. You can add a little bit of stuffing in the hand areas or use your yarn scraps, but DO NOT fill it! You want your rams to lay against the body.

Attach the gnome arms where your 12 and 36-stitch markers are.
Make sure to work in the round below the stitch marker.

ATTACH THE BEARD AND NOSE

Cut multiple 6-inch strands of your Yarn Color D. Work at stitch marker (24 sts)

Use 2 strands of yarn with your hook, hook through stitches, pull through the ends, and knot them. Attach 7 pieces in a "U" shape, starting 2 rounds below the stitch marker.

Use your yarn needle and nose tail to attach to the space created. Your nose should be attached across 3 rounds. So the bottom few beard strands will be underneath the nose.

Round 1 : MR, sc 6 (6)
Round 2: *sc inc, sc* Rep 3 (9)
Round 3 - 4: sc 9 (9)
Round 5: *sc inc, sc 2* Rep 3 (12)
Round 6 : sc 12 (12)
Round 7: *sc inc, sc 3* Rep 3 (15)
Round 8: sc 15 (15)
Round 9: *sc inc, sc 4* Rep 3 (18)
Round 10: sc 18 (18)
Round 11: *sc inc, sc 5* Rep 3 (21)
Round 12: sc 21 (21)
Round 13: *sc inc, sc 6* Rep 3 (24)
Round 14: sc 24 (24)

Round 15: *sc inc, sc 7* Rep 3 (27)
Round 16: sc 27 (27)
Round 17: *sc inc, sc 8* Rep 3 (30)
Round 18: sc 30 (30)
Round 19: *sc inc, sc 9* Rep 3 (33)
Round 20: sc 33 (33)
Round 21: *sc inc, sc 10* Rep 3 (36)
Round 22: sc 36 (36)
Round 23: *sc inc, sc 11* Rep 3 (39)
Round 24: sc 39 (39)
Round 25: *sc inc, sc 12* Rep 3 (42)
Round 26: sc 42 (42)
Round 27: *sc inc, sc 13* Rep 3 (45)
Round 28: sc 45 (45)
Round 29: *sc inc, sc 14* Rep 3 (48)
Round 30: sc 48 (48)

Flower A
Start with Yarn Color F

Round 1 : MR 6 (6)
Change to Yarn Color E
Round 2: sc inc in each st (12)
Round 3 : *ch 2, [dc inc, ch 2, sl st], sc* Rep 6

Flower B
Start with Yarn Color E
Use Yarn color D & E
Round 1 : MR 8 (8)

Change to Yarn Color D
Round 2: * [sc, ch 5, sl st] * Rep 8
Round 2: sc inc in each st (12)
Round 3 : *ch 2, [dc inc, ch 2, sl st], sc* Rep 6
Use your flower center yarn strands and sew one strand through the gnome's hat.

Simply tie the strands to secure them. Place your flowers anywhere.

Dragon Familiar

Size 9 cm
Sc-single crochet
Pr-increase, knit two from one
loop Decrease, knit two loops
with one (....)*n - what in
brackets knit the specified
number of times after the
asterisk (this is n)
Necessary materials.
~ new children's yarn main
color 15g, belly color 5g, a little
white ~ half beads eyes 5-6mm
~ padding polyester
~glue nt crystal
~ needle
~ hook 1.7
~ any other thin thread for
embroidering the muzzle
cotton
~ neodymium magnet or any
other ~ cardboard or a piece of
thin plastic for the back of the
magnet 5 by 10 cm, Body-
neck-head.

The marker goes along the
back, strictly vertically along
the back. Watch the offset.
1. In ring 6sc
2. (inc)*6=12
3. (1sc, inc)*6=18
4. (2sc, inc)*6=24
5. (3sc, inc)*6=30
6. (4sc, inc)*6=36
7- 9. 36sc (3 rows)
10. (4sc, dec)*6=30
11. (3sc, dec)*6=24
12. 24sc

Cut cardboard or plastic (I use a thin plastic backing for children's creativity) according to the
shape of the body, length for the neck is 4 cm and insert so that the body is flat from the
back. Fill your tummy a little

13. (2sc, dec)*6=18
14-18. 18sc (5 rows)
19. (2sc, dec)*4,2sc = 14
Lightly stuff the front part of the body as you knit. -2-
20-21. 14sc
22. (5sc, dec)*2=12
23-25. 12sc
Next we knit the head
26. (1sc, inc)*6=18
27. (2sc, inc)*6=24
28-34. 24sc (7 rows)
35. (2sc, dec)*6=18
36. (1sc, dec)*6=12
Lightly fill your head.
37. (dec)*6=6
Pull the loops

Dragon Familiar Continued

Muzzle.

1. Chain of 9 ch, do not close it in a ring, but knit around the chain on both sides using half
loops
2. Inc, 6sc, in one loop 4sc, on the other side 6sc, inc = 20
3. (Inc)*2, 6sc, (inc)*4, 6sc, (inc)*2 = 28
4. (1sc, inc)*2, 6sc, (1sc, inc)*4.6sc, (1sc, inc)*2=36
5-6. 36sc
7. (4sc, dec)*6=30
8. (3sc, dec)*6=24
9. (dec)*2, 4sc, (dec)*4, 4sc, (dec)*2= 16 leave thread for sewing. Stuff a little and give
shape

Decoration of the muzzle.

-Embroider the mouth as in the photo.
-The first strip is placed one row below the center row. We look at the rest from the photo.
-Make the opposite side mirrored.
-You can wrap a smile around a smile with a thread to make it more textured
-Stuff the muzzle and embroider the nostrils. Step back 3 rows from the center row. Between
the nostrils 6sc. To do this, make two stitches with a width of 2sc and wrap it with thread, just
like a smile.
-Embroider the tongue in red and the teeth in white.

-Tint the cheeks as desired.
If you are making a mouth with a drawstring, do it after sewing on the muzzle.

Breast.

We knit in turning rows. Knit tightly, without gaps
1. Chain of 4 ch
2-9. 3sc. At the end of each row do a ch rise before turning knitting
10. 1sc, inc, 1sc=4
11. 4sc
12. 1sc, inc, inc, 1sc = 6
13. Inc, 4sc, inc = 8
14-23. 8sc (10 rows)
Everyone's knitting density is different, if the chest-belly turns out to be long or shorter, you
can add
rows or remove
24. Dec, 4sc, dec=6
25. Dec, 2sc, dec =4
Sew and embroider transverse stripes as in the photo.
Sew to the bottom of the head, taking 2 rows of the neck.
Sew on after you send the chest
and belly pad
Mouth tightening. Insert the needle into the bridge of the nose, bring it into the muzzle 1 row
below the central row, grab 2-3 sc and return to the bridge of the nose. Tighten. Embroider
the mouth with contrasting thread

We knit the ears directly on the head.

Dragon Familiar Continued

Fasten the thread to the side and knit 7 ch, then knit a ss into the base loop, then 1 sc
around the head and 8 ch, fasten in the same way as the first loop. Third from 7ch
Horns.

A chain of 4 ch, we knit 3 dc back along it. Tie the horns with the remaining tails into a knot
and hide the ends in the head
Glue the eyes, embroider the whites, eyelids
at will
Tail.

1. In ring 5sc
2-3. 5sc
4-6. 3sc, 2ss=5
7. inc, 4sc=6
8. 6sc
9. (2sc, inc)*2=8
10-11. 4sc, 4ss=8
12. (3sc, inc)*2=10
13. 10sc
14-15. 5sc, 5ss=10
16. (4sc, inc)*2=12
17. 6sc, 6ss=12
18. 6sc, 1ss, 1ch, turn
19. 6sc, 1ss, 1ch, turn
20. 6sc. Leave the thread for sewing.
If desired, knit cloves along the convex edge
Fasten the thread 1sc, 2ch and ss into the base of the loop,
(2sc, 2ch and ss into the base of
the loop)* repeat until the end of the tail

Second option for attaching the tail

Feet.
1. In ka 6sc
2. (inc)*6=12
2-4. 12sc
5. (2sc, dec)*3=9
6-7. 9sc
Stuff it a little
8. (Down)*4=5 loops pull together
Embroider stitches on fingers.
Sew as in the photo
Upper paws.
1. In ring 6sc
2-10. 6sc (9 rows)
11. Fold into pieces and knit 3 sc on both sides. Leave the thread for sewing. Sew flat on the
back side so that the seam does not interfere with the magnetization of the toy. Fold the front
handles as desired

Dragon Familiar Continued

Wings.
1. Chain of 11 ch, turn
2. 10sc, ch, turn
3. 7sc, ch, turn
4. 7sc, ch, turn
5. 5sc, ch, turn
6. 5sc

If it is a magnet, stick one on the back
Niodymium (they are the strongest) If your magnet is
weak, you can stick it on your head. To
prevent the magnet from coming off the glue, you can
cover it with thin lace along the edge

Start with a slipknot

Serpent Familiar

Chain 02
Work 6 single crochet into the first chain space

Round Two
Increase
Two single crochet in each stitch (12 stitches)

Round Three
One single crochet in each stitch around

Round Four
Now work increasing
Two single crochet in the first stitch and then single crochet into the next stitch
Repeat
Increase and single crochet (18 stitches)

Round Five
One single crochet in each stitch around
Round 06
17. Two single crochet into the first stitch and then single crochet each into the next two stitches.

Serpent Familiar Continued

18. Repeat
19. Increase, single crochet and single crochet (24 stitches)
20. Round 07-10
21. Single crochet in each stitch around for four rows.

Round 11
23. (6 Decreases) that's one single crochet in two stitches together
24. Lets do invisible decreases in which the hook is only being put through the font loops
25. Do 06 decreases.
26. Work 12 single crochet for the rest of the row.

Round 12
28. Invisible decrease and single crochet
29. Repeat all the way around for R12.
30. Add stuffing

Round 13
Decrease > four single crochet > Decrease > four single crochets

Rounds 14-67
34. One single crochet in each and every stitch around for each Round.
35. Now the body is ready
36. It is time for making the tail you will be making decreases.
37. Round 68
38. Decrease > 03 Single Crochets > Decrease > 03 Single Crochets
39. Round 69
40. 02 Single Crochets > Decrease > 02 Single Crochets > Decrease
41. Round 70
42. 06 single crochets
43. Add stuffing

Round 71
45. Decrease > Single Crochet > Decrease > Single Crochet

Cut the Yarn
47. Now place the eye with thread. You can also use Google Eye / Safety Eyes.

Counted Cross Stitch Samples

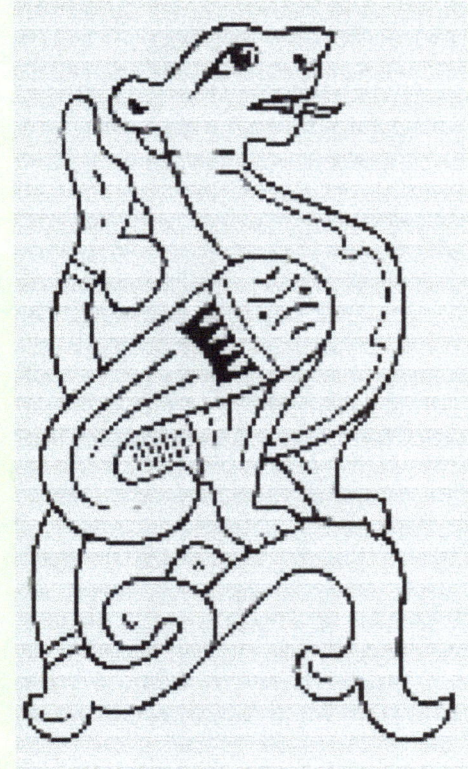

Fayte is a queer Trans Non-Binary knitter who resides in the beautiful Pacific Northwest of Canada home to the ancestral and unceded territories of the xʷməθkʷəy̓əm (Musqueam), Sḵwx̱wú7mesh (Squamish), and səlilwətaɬ (Tsleil-Waututh) Nations. Fayte lives with their fantastic cat Noodle who is 11 years young and a constant inspiration to the writing process. As a witch Fayte draws on their ancestors from Slavic origin to guide them through their process. They believe it is the master weavers, seamstresses, and knitters in their lineage who shared the cosmic knowledge of knitting magic with them. It is their hope you find comfort and knowledge in their writing.

The Three Little Sisters

The Three Little Sisters is an indie publisher that puts authors first. We specialize in the strange and unusual. From titles about pagan and heathen spirituality to traditional fiction we bring books to life.

https://shop.the3littlesisters.com

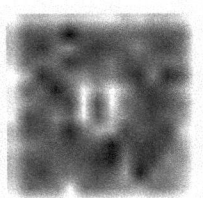